THE FAMILY THAT *LAUGHS TOGETHER ....*

A Quick Guide to Sanity When You Feel Like Screaming

Roberta Gold, R.T.C., CHP

Laughter Rocks!

Published by:

Laughter for the Health of It

laf4u@sbcglobal.net

Publishing consultant:

Professional Woman Publishing, LLC

www.pwnbooks.com

ISBN: 978-0-578-20309-6

This book is dedicated to my incredible children
Ted Jonathan and Devorah Gina
who continue to inspire me to be the best parent I can be.

Contents

Acknowledgements:

This book has been a labor of love in my mission to create a generation of happier, more resilient youth and happier, more relaxed and engaged parents and teachers.

I feel very blessed to have parents who raised me with love and laughter and a brother who has laughed with me (and at me) throughout my life! They instilled in me a sense of wonder and awe that has fueled my life. I can not thank my parents and brother enough!

Linda Eastman was my book coach and I thank her for being a wonderful sounding board as well as my cheerleader. I want to thank Kerry Harr and Jen Smith for reading and critiquing my final copy – their insight and suggestions were invaluable.

I am very grateful for the love and support of my husband and wonderful family who provide me with reasons to laugh and enjoy life every day!

I believe that we can change the world
if we raise resilient, happy children!

I believe children can learn to have a positive attitude!

I believe children can learn to focus on the strengths of others!

I believe that changing our attitudes will result in happier children!

I believe laughter is an equalizer!

I believe parents, teachers, grandparents
are a child's biggest influencers!

I believe we can change the world
if we raise resilient, happy children!

We need to be 16 years of age and pass a written and driving test to get your drivers license. We have to be 21 years of age (in the United States) to legally go into a bar and buy an alcoholic drink. We need to take classes and get a diploma before applying for most jobs. Yet, anyone can have a child!

Being a parent is one of the hardest jobs in the world. However there are no mandatory classes to take, diplomas to get, and no license is required. The majority of first time parents are overwhelmed, overworked and overstressed. **Humor** and **laughter** are tools that will help!

We start with the best intentions to teach our children to have happy and productive lives. Somewhere along the way we may forget to teach them the happy part. That's the part I feel we need to start teaching early so they will learn how to find joy in simple things - in nature, with their friends, in school, by themselves and with family.

Parents are a child's first teacher and it's never too late for a parent to learn new tricks. These new tricks can bring your family back to calm and peace instead of stressed and frazzled. Incorporating a little bit of silly into family life can make life in general much more pleasant and a whole lot less stressful.

Being a "Silly" mom or dad is what we can strive for. Silly, meaning *childlike* not childish. Childish is always joking around, being immature or playing practical jokes with your kids. Childlike and silly are about being light hearted and having a positive attitude, learning to see the humorous side of situations that could easily anger or frustrate us. Being a silly parent means setting a good example for our kids on how to handle so many of life's challenges. It also means helping our children learn to laugh, especially at themselves, instead of internalizing the negative self deprecating feelings many kids have if things go wrong.

Anger, frustration, disappointment, jealousy and being hurt are all natural emotions. However, these are the emotions we tend to try to brush aside, not to deal with, not allow to be talked about because that may be too painful for us as well as our children. If we can teach our kids how to actively deal with these genuine emotions, in a productive way that does not harm them or anyone else, we may enable open, honest discussions of their feelings. If we find our child not wanting to talk about what is bothering them, perhaps offer to watch a movie or play a game or take a walk or bake cookies with them. They most likely still want us to be there with them, even if they don't want to talk right then.

I have found that if we can look at a situation and are able to find some humor in it, any little bit of humor, then we can talk about it, deal with it and move on from it. Humor is one way to deal with all of these valid emotions!

Society today is very complex and demanding; most of our lives are rushed and we are always running somewhere. We can easily get caught up in the hustle-bustle of all the work we have and become overwhelmed. Our kids model our behavior; they sense when we are uptight, when we are annoyed, and when we have a short fuse. They do not always react to our moods in the way we would like. Most of the time it's when we are at our own wit's end that our children choose to have their own crisis. This is the moment when we parents have to stop and find some humor.

We can be the role model for an attitude adjustment. It may be hard at first, but it will eventually become so easy you will be amazed! All it takes is a little practice. And what could be more fun than learning how to have more levity in life?

Here are 11 simple ways to help see the bright side of life and to help our families have more fun.

CHAPTER 1

Learn to Laugh at Yourself

I am always bumping into something or tripping over nothing, just stumbling as I walk. I realize that it must look funny to anyone watching me. I have learned to laugh as soon as I stumble and to quickly look around and blame it on the dog, the couch, the chair, or anything around me. I exaggerate it for effect. My children now expect this from me and have even started helping me come up with who or what may have caused me to trip. We all end up laughing together. My daughter blames me whenever she stumbles, hits her elbow on a door handle, or stubs her toe on a chair. She just brushes it off with a loud, "Thanks, Mom!"

I try to look for the funny side of things everywhere and in everything. It is so easy to see the negativity in our world—just turn on the news or read the current headlines. It is much more difficult to find absurdity in our day to day activities, but the hilarity is there. The first place to find humor is *within* ourselves, learning to laugh at our own little missteps - things we say wrong, hear wrong, or do wrong - is the beginning of being able to spot comical happenings all around us.

When I trip over nothing, I find that if I say something fast and laugh first, people will laugh with me instead of at me. When we say something witty about our own mishaps, it eases those around us. We are human and have a tendency to react to other's discomfort and be embarrassed for them. By saying something to make others laugh, we release their tension and everyone laughs together. There have been many famous people throughout history who have had the witty gift of fast comebacks – from actors and comedians to politicians to literary writers - such as Winston Churchill, Mark Twain, Mae West, George Bernard Shaw, Groucho Marx, Oscar Wilde, Margaret Thatcher. These were people who were able to respond with fast one liners that deflected anything potentially humiliating to them. You may know people who can do this as well.

Don't worry if you are not so quick. Many comebacks are sarcastic and we need to be careful to say something that pokes fun at ourselves and does not put others down. There are many things we can do instead. One easy way is to start laughing at ourselves whenever we can. When we start taking ourselves less seriously, it can make it easier to react with a laugh, which will then make it easier to start observing all the humor around us. We will also find that we start noticing all the good happening instead of all the bad, which I feel is a much healthier way to look at life. One of the ways that has helped me find the humor is by watching people and animals. I can always find mirth in how they interact and react to situations they find themselves in. This helps us see humor in some of the awkward situations we may find ourselves in and hopefully allows us to laugh out loud. When our children watch us react with humor and laughter to situations that could be emotionally uncomfortable, it gives them a great tool to use for the embarrassing situations in which they may find themselves. Wouldn't it be better for our children to see us laugh when we trip over nothing, rather than scream?

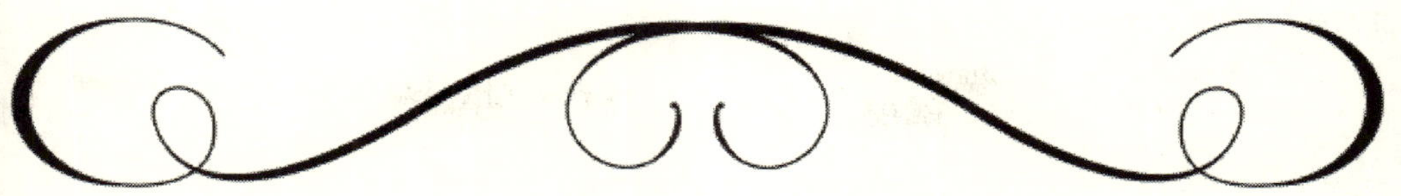

Learn to nurture your "Humor Bone".

Our "Humor Bone" starts in our head and

runs through our entire body.

Our "Humor Bone" is the way we look at the world.

By nurturing it we learn to look for the humor all around us.

And we laugh much more.

Time for Self Reflection:

What do you remember that was so funny it would cause you to laugh out loud when you were a child?

____

____

____

Can you recall laughing at any mishap you had? Describe what happened and how you were able to find it humorous.

____

____

____

What did your parents, grandparents or other adults around you laugh about when you were growing up?

____

____

____

CHAPTER 2

Laugh at the Little Annoyances

I was cooking dinner one night and spent more than three hours prepping the chicken, chopping the veggies, making the dressing, and setting the table. As I was carrying the dish to put it in the oven, I tripped and it spilled onto the floor. All the work I had put into preparing the meal was gone in a split second. I almost started crying until I looked up and saw our dog staring at the contents all over the floor with the biggest smile on her face, looking like she had just won the lottery. I started laughing — hysterically laughing — and couldn't stop. The kids and my husband thought I had gone nuts, but before long they too started laughing.

What could have been a disaster and made me angry, instead made me laugh and resulted in my children laughing and realizing that when you cannot control something, laughing about it is better than getting angry. There wasn't anything I could do about the meal after it fell; getting angry would not bring the meal back.

Laughing out loud and making sure our children see us laughing is a great way to set the example of being lighthearted. They sure see us when we are angry or upset. We should teach them how to find humor in things that would otherwise disturb them so they learn to laugh about these things, such as these irritating examples:

- Waiting in line for one item in the 10 items or less line and the person in front of us has at least 50 items
- Having a screaming child sit right next to us at a restaurant
- Being cut off in traffic by a rude driver
- Missing our airline flight by only 5 minutes and having to take the next flight 3 hours later
- Waiting for the person in front of the line to find the ticket to the movie he put "somewhere"
- Putting up with the person yelling their conversation into their cell phone

All of these situations can be viewed in a different way if we use our humor bone. When we make an effort to look for the humor in them, and engage our children to look as well, we bond as we agree on what is funny about the annoying things others are doing.

Laughing out loud, especially exaggerating the laughing, is cathartic. Set an example by being able to laugh about situations over which we have no control; model for our children how to brush things off of us, how to not sweat the small stuff. Being able to roll with things that come up by laughing instead of reacting negatively shows children how to cope when things do not turn out as planned. Also, by laughing out loud, we are sure to have others join in since laughter is very contagious!

Practice laughing! Go ahead and try it, right now. Just start laughing. I guarantee if there are other people around, you will not be laughing alone for long. If you don't feel comfortable doing this yet, try laughing alone until you feel at ease enough to try it in front of your children. Next, take this practice out in public and see what happens. The more we practice laughing, the easier it will be to react with laughter instead of anger. To help get the laughter started, watch videos of laughing babies and funny animals. Two minutes of watching babies laugh should get you going yourself. Just remember we should never hide our laughter. When we laugh, we share it!

Keep in mind, there are certain things that can not be changed once they happen – the dinner I made was ruined – however I was then able to offer my family the choice of pizza or burgers, and they were happy, almost as happy as my dog!

It is when we least feel like laughing that we should be laughing. If we fake our laughter and just start laughing, our body will not know we are faking it and will react by releasing our body's tension and pains. As we are actually physically laughing out loud, it is impossible to be mad, angry, stressed, or depressed. These are mutually opposite emotions.

Time for Self Reflection:

What made you laugh out loud when you were growing up?
TV shows? Friends? Siblings? A joke you heard? Something you did? Something you saw another do?

____

____

____

Who in your family can you remember had a really great laugh?

____

____

____

What made their laugh so great?

____

____

____

CHAPTER 3

Break Up Your Routine

My favorite day of the year is April Fool's Day. This is the day I look forward to all year. I plan out how I am going to surprise my family. One year, when my children were still in elementary school, I made them a special breakfast and set the table with a beautiful potted plant in the center. When they sat down, I served them perfectly cooked sunny-side up eggs, toast cut into smiley faces, and jungle juice to start their day off right! I sat down with them and immediately grabbed some of the rocks (actually chocolate rocks sitting in ground up Oreo dirt) in the potted plant and, to my children's horror, ate them. They tried to eat their eggs only to find out they were gummy eggs. The jungle juice was a mixture of orange, cranberry, and guava with chopped green mint floating around so it looked silly. We all had a good laugh and they reported they had the best day ever at school – retelling their breakfast meal to their friends!

Changing up the day to day routine will keep your family from complaining of boredom. I actually never allowed my children to say they were bored. I challenged them to find things to do when they had free time, whether it was playing solitaire, word games, puzzles, going outside for a few minutes, or calling a friend. It didn't matter as long as they found something to occupy their time. Creating lists of things your children enjoy helps when they just can't think of anything to do. Encourage *them* to think of the things they like to do. We can start the brainstorming if needed, but make sure we are not the ones creating the list. Our child's participation will better help them remember what they enjoy doing and will build their confidence. Be sure to support their ideas.

Changing up the daily routine can be really fun. We can surprise our family or have them help decide what kind of day we will all have. Here are some suggestions my family has enjoyed for using humor on any day, in many ways:

- Tell jokes – even ones not yet memorized but written down.
- Look for belly button lint.
- Have a backwards day, hat day, no shoes day, eat breakfast for dinner day or vice-versa, etc.
- Make happy face pancakes to start the day.
- Once in awhile, say yes to dessert before dinner.

- Wear bright colors.
- Sing a silly song when you wake the kids up for school or put them to bed.
- Read your kids a funny book of silly poems.
- Play a comedy CD or put on the comedy channel in the car - there are many for kids as well as teens and adults.
- Put a written joke in your kids' lunch bags.
- Make crazy shaped pasta.

By being creative and using our imagination, it is surprising how exciting it is just thinking of ways to have fun during a regular school / work week.

Doing something out of the ordinary breaks the regularly expected daily schedule, and it doesn't have to just be once a year, it can be any day of the week. My family tries to outdo each other with funny pranks and special silly days. My children are now the ones who come up with the great April Fool's Day ideas!

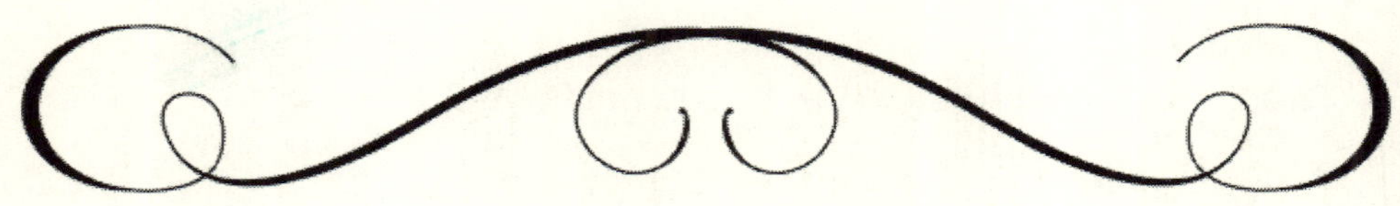

No one has ever liked change.

Most people remain where they are due to not wanting to change anything. Yet, it is impossible to grow if we do not accept change. One of the best things we can help our children do is to go with the flow, be able to adapt to new and challenging situations that pop up in their lives.

And to find the humor so we can laugh along the way.

Time for Self Reflection:

Can you remember having to change plans that you were really looking forward to? Was it easy to change those plans or did you resist? Describe what happened.

___

___

___

How could you have handled the situation differently if you were able to just brush it off and go with something else?

___

___

___

What are some are your favorite things to do with your family?

___

___

___

CHAPTER 4

Share the Humor

One Mother's Day, after a wonderful dinner with my husband, children, mother, father, brother, sister-in-law, niece and nephew, my mother pulled out envelopes for all of us. To our surprise, she had cut out a cartoon from the newspaper that she felt related to each one of us. We laughed as we read them and then passed them around to each other. We loved the cartoons and agreed that she had captured each of us perfectly with the ones she chose. It started a tradition that we still continue today.

I am always trying to find ways to spread humor with our family. I started a Humor File when the kids were babies, collecting everything and anything that made me laugh. It started with one file folder and became so big I had to start organizing it into multiple folders. I could then pull something out — a cartoon, a joke, a ridiculous picture, a saying — and post it somewhere.

Having a central area where everyone looks every day, like the refrigerator or bathroom mirror, keeps everyone on alert to look for humor. Post things for the whole family to see. It is important to keep it fresh so change the item daily or weekly. When my kids started to ask about it, I had them help me find humorous items to post. Make *maintaining the silly* a family affair.

Here are some other ideas we found worked well:

- Point out funny things when you see them, (unless it Involves making fun of others).
- Find humor that does not belittle.
- Discover humor in nature, in animals, and in objects.
- Look online as well as in the newspaper or magazines for cartoons, headlines that are funny, want ads, and personals. Look twice at the regular news stories — sometimes there is humor and irony in the way they are written.
- Signs on billboards, buildings or stores can be misprinted and seem silly.
- Restaurant menus can have funny wording.

Nothing is safe from humor; it is all around us and often shows up in ordinary ways. To this day, I still add to my Humor Files and continue to find cartoons that relate to members of my family and friends. I enjoy re-finding things in my files that make me laugh again and again!

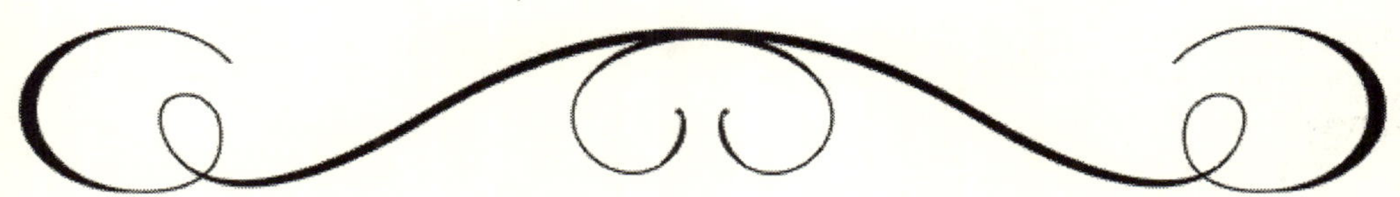

Write down things you hear that made you laugh.

Take pictures of anything you see that gives you a chuckle.

Our brains have so much to process that we easily forget the simple things that give us pleasure in the moment. Luckily we can capture these moments and watch them over and over again.

Time for Self Reflection:

Where do you find things to laugh about?

____

____

____

How were you encouraged to laugh as a child? Or was laughter not allowed in your home and why?

____

____

____

Describe the last really great laughter induced time you had? Who were you with? What were you doing? How did you feel?

____

____

____

CHAPTER 5

Encourage the Silliness

My husband loves classic comedy shows and movies – Three Stooges and Jerry Lewis movies are his favorites. He turned my children on to them when they were young; they, in turn, had their friends watch the movies and TV shows with them. This also happens with other humorous movies and TV shows we have watched together. We can say one line and then just break out laughing, remembering the scene and putting it into the context of the moment! For instance, we love the movie The Mask, starring Jim Carey. All we have to do is say "Smokin" and we break out laughing – even if it has nothing related to what we are talking about. It breaks ups the moment and brings needed levity into whatever we are talking about! Now we all use one-liners to punctuate something we are saying and we all laugh together.

We can encourage our child's humor development by rewarding them for their laughter. When we sit down to dinner, the first thing I ask everyone is "What made you laugh today" "What did you do that was fun today" This will help everyone begin to think of the good things in their day. Be careful never to put them down for being "silly" and let them know it is okay to laugh, tell jokes and share humorous times. This brings us closer as a family and we become more comfortable laughing out loud, spotting humorous things and situations, and our children are more willing to share silly times with us.

Teaching our kids about the great comedians of our times by watching old comedies and sitcoms together and explaining to them how we laughed growing up with these, will help them to think of comedians in a positive way. A few things we can try with our family may be:

- Having Joke Nights
- Comedy Hours
- Humor Fests

These will encourage everyone to share something they find funny. Be sure the kids know that everything is fair game, that there is no right or wrong to what makes them laugh (as long as it doesn't hurt or belittle anyone else). Persuade everyone to come up with ideas for special family humor times. Try using a line from a movie or TV show, it could start a family laugh.

Use your television as a connector instead of a baby sitter. Choose TV shows or movies that you can watch together with the family. Talk about how the characters used humor in certain situations. Asking our children what they thought were the best parts of the show is an easy way we can connect with them.

Time for Self Reflection:

Who was your favorite comedian(s) when you were young?

____

____

____

Who are the comedians that can make you break out laughing now?

____

____

____

What are some TV shows and or movies you remember watching as a child that even thinking of them can conjure up smiles and laughs?

____

____

____

What funny shows or movies do you watch with your family now?

____

____

____

CHAPTER 6

Show Them You Continue to Be Silly

My son has now graduated from college and lives and works in another state. I still send him "care" packages for his birthday, holidays, and just because. I don't send traditional items, though; I hunt around for things that remind me of my son growing up. I send miniature table tennis sets, funny PEZ dispensers, Lego sets, whoopee cushions, magic tricks, board games, cartoon books, comic books, Silly Putty, and anything else that strikes my "Humor Bone." Even though my son has come to expect these care packages from me, he never tires of getting them and says he loves that I can still surprise him. He tells his friends about the silly gifts I send and opens the packages in front of them so they can share in the laughs. I make sure there are items that he can engage in with his friends as well.

I give humorous gifts for birthdays, graduations, good grades on tests, happy first days of spring, for any occasion, or for any reason at all. Being creative and thinking of appropriate items that will cause a laugh is so much fun. For example, when my teenage daughter had trouble with friends, I gave her a Magic 8 Ball, started asking it questions, and then laughed at the answers it gave. I gave my young son a basketball with a smiley face on it, and let him know that it wouldn't matter if he makes a basket or not, the ball will always be happy with him. I give items with smiley faces on them to everyone.

I am also always on a search for humorous items. My children (and friends) have come to expect me to find things that make me laugh. My daughter now tells me about stores that have things I may want to give out. She is actually doing what I do, nurturing her "Humor Bone" and seeking out the funny, without even realizing it. Searching and looking for humorous items is as much fun as finding them because it puts you into a positive frame of mind. I don't need a reason to buy things that put a smile on my face and create laughs for others.

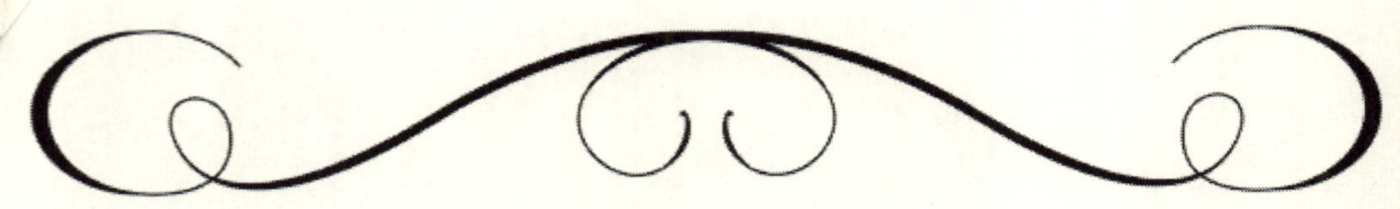

Go on humor hunts.

Make it a family affair and something exciting.

Get everyone revved up for the hunt by building it up for a day or two beforehand. Then have the kids help decide where to go to search. You may also have gift creating times. Drawing, writing favorite sayings or song lyrics, anything that can be done by hand would be great ways to show how to give gifts from the heart that don't cost anything.

Time for Self Reflection:

What gifts can you give (or have you given) that don't cost any money but generate smiles and laughs?

____

____

____

What was something you received that still draws your smile when you look at it?

____

____

____

Where might you be able to go to find items that would cause someone to laugh or at least smile?

____

____

____

CHAPTER 7

Plan Family Fun Days and Nights

Our family enjoys a domino game called Mexican Train. We have been known to stay up into the wee hours of the night to finish one game. While playing it, we now have rituals that invoke laughter. My brother always asks how many dominos we take and my sister-in-law and I like to use objects to help us reach the dominos – such as an enormous bag of pistachios or a long metal back scratcher. It is more how we use these objects that are funny, such as using them to reach the tiles clearly within our arm's reach – it is just so much more fun to use a bag of pistachios! There is also always someone who doesn't know it is their turn and someone who makes their move too fast, skipping someone else's turn. We know these things are going to happen and laugh at the anticipation of them! Although this game, as well as some of the others, can become very competitive, if you play with the aim to have fun, it doesn't matter who wins. The main objects are togetherness and fun!

Play games! There are so many nights (and days) when all we want to d_ come home, sit in front of the television, and zone out. This may seem like a great escape from the hectic pace of the day, but it actually won't de-stress us as much as a fun game will. With a game, you interact in many ways – talking, sportsmanship, teamwork if there are teams involved, discussions and reflections of memories that naturally come to mind or remind you of a certain fun time. Encourage the silliness when you play games and be sure to laugh out loud.

We like to be together as a family and share rowdy games of cards, Monopoly, Twister, Scattergories, Pictionary, Taboo, Chicken Foot or any of the other wonderful, laughter inspiring games out there. My family expects games now. Even though my children are older, when they come home, one of the first things they do is pull out a deck of cards. Playing games creates fun, conversation, and most of all, laughter! It doesn't really matter which games, only that when engaged in them we relax, let loose, and laugh together.

A playful parent is the best kind of parent.

In a perfect world we would always be in a good mood, our kids would always listen to us and behave as we wish they would. Unfortunately we do not live in a perfect world, nor should we. When we learn how to put ourselves into a playful mood, we find that the stresses of the day melt away. We discover we have more fun and in turn have more fun with our children. Playing games helps to get the fun going when we may think we are too worn out to do anything.

Time for Self Reflection:

What family (or friends) games were you playing while growing up? Puzzles? Cards? Board Games? Street Games?

___

___

___

What games are you playing with your family now? (Or wish you were playing?)

___

___

___

What other ways can you play with your children?

___

___

___

CHAPTER 8

Go With the Unexpected

Whenever we go out to dinner with my brother and sister-in-law, invariably my sister-in-law's order comes back different than as she ordered it. This has happened over and over to the point that we now joke about it before it happens and become almost hysterical with laughter when the waiter delivers the dish. We can anticipate the order coming out wrong and laugh about it even as we are deciding where to have dinner. Now if we go somewhere and the order actually arrives correctly as ordered, we are somewhat disappointed and laugh about that too!

There are always going to be things that happen that irritate us, that are not right, and that end up different than planned. When things like this happen repeatedly, it can be disheartening — if we let it be. There may not be much we can do about a situation except to anticipate it and then laugh about it later. This can translate to other situations and people as well, such as people who are irritating, or times when nothing goes right.

Of course we do need to help our children see that some things are beyond our control. However, we can show them how to deflect disappointment and see the brighter side of situations that appear disastrous. There will always be people that anger us - don't give them that power. Try picturing them as a cartoon character, like Goofy, and realize they are not going to respond as we might like. Doing this makes it easier to stay calm, say what needs to be said, and move on with the day with the least amount of damage to our bodies.

We cannot change another person or situation; we only have the ability to change our own reaction. In these moments, if we can find something funny to laugh about, it will reduce our stress. Make the negative a positive and something to look forward to. For example, now when we are deciding where to dine, we often say, "Let's go to the Café, we know they will botch up Lori's order there!"

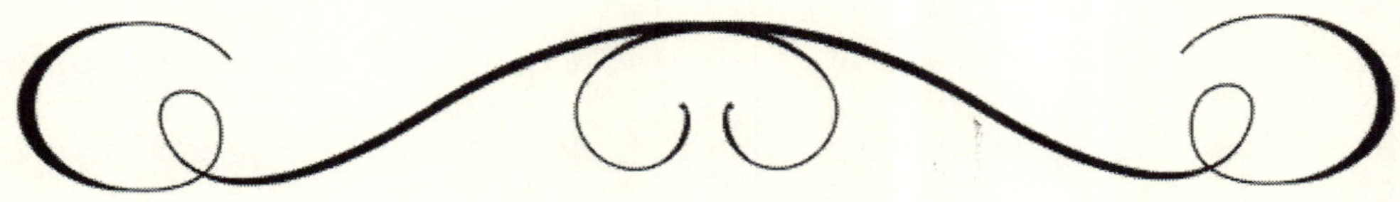

We do not have the ability to change someone else. The best psychiatrist in the world can not change another person; they have to want to change. We only have the ability to change our own perspective so we can deal with that individual (or situation) with the least amount of damage to ourselves.

Time for Self Reflection:

What happened recently that really set you off? And how did you react?

____

____

____

How can you revisit the situation and find some humor in it?

____

____

____

CHAPTER 9

Create Laughter Memories

The night before my son graduated from elementary school he decided to bleach his brown hair blonde. He looked like a totally different child. I had no time to tell my extended family before they came to see him graduate. My brother came up to me after the graduation and said he took many pictures and got some great shots. He, of course, did not know my son had dyed his hair. When my son came up to all of us afterwards, my brother started laughing — he had taken great pictures of some other child. The memory carried on to when my son graduated from high school and college; my brother made sure my son still looked the same before taking pictures. We still laugh about it today!

Sometimes we go about our day and expect things to be a certain way. When they don't go as planned, we tend to become angry, irritated, and upset. We may instantly react in a negative way – either lashing out at ourselves or whoever comes near us first.

Our children learn from our reactions. When unexpected situations occur, it's important that we stop, take a moment to step back, and look at the situation from a different perspective. Find the humor in it and accept that it's done and there is nothing we can change about it. Then maybe we can learn to laugh instead of yell. There are studies showing that our children have higher stress levels because they react to our stress more than anything else in their lives. By learning how to see the humor in the situations we have no control over changing, we can calm down and deal with what needs to be dealt with in a rational way. I didn't end up with any pictures of my son's elementary school graduation. I did, however, gain a great tale to tell.

Not everything you face can be changed.

But nothing can be changed that isn't faced.

Humor and laughter help you face difficult situations

so you can deal with them and move on.

Time for Self Reflection:

Think about your day or your week, are you bringing home the stress into your household? In what ways do we add to what may already be a stressful day?

____

____

____

What are some of your top stressors?

Work demands? Inconsiderate co-worker or neighbor?
Traffic and foolish drivers? Money issues?
Or the tiny day to day minutia that just build up?

____

____

____

What can you do to leave the stress outside and bring levity into your home to change the atmosphere?

____

____

____

CHAPTER 10

Balance their Differences

My children have always had different approaches to their school work and tests. My daughter has always been very hard on herself, wanting to get top grades, stressing over projects and tests and always giving her very best. My son on the other hand was more interested in getting to know all the teachers and counselors on campus. One year when I picked them up from school they had received their report cards. My daughter almost throws hers at me. I looked and saw all A's and one B+. She was very upset. I said, "Honey this is a great report card!" In a rather angry voice she points to the B and says, "That was supposed to be an A!" My son hands me his report card with a, "Hey, I passed!"

Those of us who have more than one child know that no matter how hard we try, they will develop into their own beings and we just have to learn how to help them become more balanced, to be healthy, happy children.

As I have said previously, we need to be role models. We need to show our children how to achieve balance in their lives. I know that this is extremely hard for most of us who may struggle with our own lack of time or resources to be able to do what we really wish we could do. If we can do one thing per day that brings us joy, that is a start. And by focusing on our joys we show our families that things are okay.

When you have a child that is very hard on themselves and in turn may snap or be short with you when they are stressed, it is difficult to maintain your calm. Most often we tend to get sucked in to their stress and react with anger or sharpness ourselves. This only makes matters worse as we know. If we can stop ourselves and wait until we can be supportive, then we may be able to bring our child into a calmer place. This is when we need to think of something that makes us laugh, anything that you can conjure up – a funny image from the past, something someone said that made you laugh, or that cartoon character you like. The key is to maintain our inner calm instead of getting caught up in their battle.

The reverse is also true. When we have a nonchalant child, one who appears not to care what happens, this can cause us to want to pull our hair out as well. We try everything to get them motivated to finish their homework or complete their projects, to the point of loosing our control. We need to step back and realize that this child may be bored with the work or may be frustrated with it, but they do not share these feelings. Finding ways to engage them so they feel it is fun doing the work may be helpful. Here are some things I have used with my children:

- Pick up an object near by and make it talk, make it be silly.
- Tell your child to stop working, that you agree it is senseless. Tell them to go out and get a job instead of school.
- Talk in a silly voice and say silly things not related to the conversation.
- Offer to have a tea party instead of homework

Doing something that enables us to become calm, (finding a way to laugh) will help so we are not over reactive. It will also help our child change their mood so they may be able to find ways to finish the work they need to do.

My children have graduated from great universities and are both doing quite well. My son works very hard at his profession, giving it his all, and loving what he does. He is able to let things that bother him (and there are things that get him really heated up,) roll off quicker, to turn his anger into a smile and to recover faster when someone does something that annoys him. My daughter has never waivered in her need to do her best and get top grades. She still pushes herself in everything she does, stressing over what is important to her. However, she has learned to find ways to relax more and to make time to have fun.

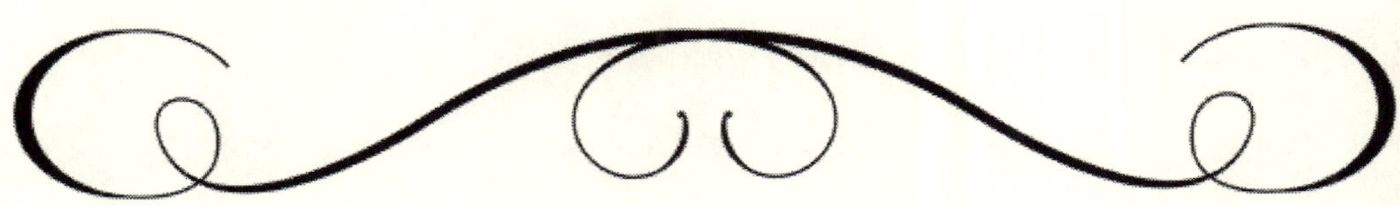

We are only as happy as our most miserable child. This intensifies as our children get older and their problems grow as well. There was actually a study that confirmed this (did we need one?) Humor and laughter help us parents gain perspective so we do not feed into our child's unhappiness.

Time for Self Reflection:

Why sweat the small stuff? Describe how you can get yourself into a new mindset that allows you to see the ridiculous of the situation?

____

____

____

What is your go to image or saying or whatever that can change your mood and make you smile and laugh?

____

____

____

CHAPTER 11

Attitude is Everything

My daughter loved being naked when she was quite young. It amazed me how fast she could take off her clothes. I would help her get dressed so we could go out and as soon as we were ready to leave the house she would be naked. It seemed to happen when we were already running behind and I was getting stressed because we were going to be late. I would feel like screaming. My son had his own ways to feed into my most harried times, they were more subtle yet just as effective in throwing me into a tizzy.

Does your child have tantrums? Mine have never had a tantrum last longer than about 15 seconds. Want to learn how? When my child started yelling or crying or fussing about something and did not respond to anything I said, that is when I would change the scene. I would do something that they would least expect. My favorite was to start clapping as I said, "Yeah!! You are doing exactly what you should!" They would usually stop screaming at this and give me a look like I was bonkers. I would then look at my watch or the clock and say, "Yes that's right. It is actually no smile time now," and of course this would make them smile or even laugh. "No. No smiling. No laughing. Stop that right now." We always ended up laughing together and the tantrum was over super fast. As my children got older and I continued to use this method to break them out of their tirades, they would tell me, "Stop mom. I don't want to laugh right now," which was fine since it still worked to change their mood. This technique works with any person of any age. If we can do something that is completely out of the ordinary and unexpected, we can stop the negative behavior in order to calm the person down. I have actually used this when a colleague was out of control. All I had to do was say something absurd such as, "Great, the green goblins come here in 10 minutes, will you greet them?" The person (or child) upset, stops, looks at me like I am crazy and is able to calm down and talk about why they were upset.

We don't want our kids to grow up and become stressed out frazzled adults, yet studies show that children's stress is directly related to their parent's stress. We need to find ways to brush off the small stuff, roll with the unexpected, see the possible humor in it, so we don't over react and are able to step back and find a way to get through it all. We can role model for our children a healthy way to live. It makes family life easier and much more fun, and makes the future for them (and us) a whole lot brighter.

When my daughter had all her clothes off, I would pull myself together as best I could and try humor. I might take her dress and start putting it on her doll or teddy bear saying, "This is now your dress Miss Dollie since she does not want to wear it any more." Usually my daughter would come over and put it on. Humor helps!

There are times we need to hit our own reset button. We need to pause, take a deep breath, and walk away. If we remember not to react but to step back and take time to reflect before reacting, we will be able to restore our equilibrium before taking action. We will then be modeling healthy emotional responses to what may otherwise have triggered our anger.

Time for Self Reflection:

What does your child or children do that seem to always push your buttons?

____

____

____

What can you do to reframe those feelings?

____

____

____

How can you bring humor into those situations when you feel you are going to lose it?

____

____

____

Life can be hard enough. We don't have to add to the stress. We can make it easier on ourselves and our kids by finding ways to laugh, every day. It is easier than we may think to make shifts in how we behave. Start small. Start silly. If this is new territory, our children may be very surprised at first but believe me, they won't complain when Mom or Dad decides to laugh instead of yell!

My hope is that this little guide book will provide the spark you may need. That it will enable you to nurture your "Humor Bone" and see new ways to have fun with your family and friends. By finding enjoyable ways to reduce the stress caused by our crazy world and allowing us to slow down and take delight in life's simple pleasures, we are doing good for our family. Remember that no matter how hard we try, our children may still want to have their tantrum or may want to sulk alone or may want to continue to push our buttons. It hurts to see our kids unhappy, however, resist the urge to fix everything for them. Instead, facilitate ways for them to roll with life's ups and downs so they can reduce their own stress and laugh. My wish is that we set an example for our children so they will turn out to be the happy, healthy, resilient adults we envision for them!

We choose how we react to life's situations. Let's choose to find the humor. The family that laughs together......have a whole lot more fun!

You now have the tools to put into action what you have learned. Are you ready for the 21 Day Laughter Challenge?

The 21 Day Laughter Challenge has a daily journal for you to keep track of how you are practicing what you have learned.

I want to invite you to be part of our private book page on my Laughter Rocks! Website: www.laughterrocks.org

Password is: Book848

You can post your self reflections and your journal entries. I will give you feedback and if you choose, you can get feedback from other readers.

Think about some of these as you make your journal entries:

- What are you doing with your family?
- Are you having laughter fests? Crazy, silly days?
- How did you lighten up?
- Have your children responded differently to your lighter self? How?
- Has the mood in your home changed?
- Are you finding it easier to laugh when you had wanted to scream?
- Most of all, try to find what works for you and your family and write it down so you can refer to it when needed.

Day 1 of the 21 Day Laughter Challenge

Date: ____________________

What challenged your equilibrium today? What was your attitude? How did you over come it? Was it easy it lighten up? How did your family react? What did you learn today?

____

____

____

____

____

____

____

____

____

____

____

____

____

____

Day 2 of the 21 Day Laughter Challenge

Date: ____________________

What challenged your equilibrium today? What was your attitude? How did you over come it? Was it easy it lighten up? How did your family react? What did you learn today?

Day 3 of the 21 Day Laughter Challenge

Date: ____________________

What challenged your equilibrium today? What was your attitude? How did you over come it? Was it easy it lighten up? How did your family react? What did you learn today?

____

____

____

____

____

____

____

____

____

____

____

____

____

____

Day 4 of the 21 Day Laughter Challenge

Date: ____________________

What challenged your equilibrium today? What was your attitude? How did you over come it? Was it easy it lighten up? How did your family react? What did you learn today?

Day 5 of the 21 Day Laughter Challenge

Date: ____________________

Hooray! You made it a forth of the way! Do you feel this is going well? Why or why not?

What challenged your equilibrium today? What was your attitude? How did you over come it? Was it easy it lighten up? How did your family react? What did you learn today?

___

___

___

___

___

___

___

___

___

___

___

___

Day 6 of the 21 Day Laughter Challenge

Date: ____________________

What challenged your equilibrium today? What was your attitude? How did you over come it? Was it easy it lighten up? How did your family react? What did you learn today?

Day 7 of the 21 Day Laughter Challenge

Date: ____________________

What challenged your equilibrium today? What was your attitude? How did you over come it? Was it easy it lighten up? How did your family react? What did you learn today?

Day 8 of the 21 Day Laughter Challenge

Date: ____________________

What challenged your equilibrium today? What was your attitude? How did you over come it? Was it easy it lighten up? How did your family react? What did you learn today?

____

____

____

____

____

____

____

____

____

____

____

____

____

____

Day 9 of the 21 Day Laughter Challenge

Date: ____________________

What challenged your equilibrium today? What was your attitude? How did you over come it? Was it easy it lighten up? How did your family react? What did you learn today?

Day 10 of the 21 Day Laughter Challenge

Date: ____________________

Yahoo, you are half way there! Are you seeing changes in your family? In what ways?

What challenged your equilibrium today? What was your attitude? How did you over come it? Was it easy it lighten up? How did your family react? What did you learn today?

____

____

____

____

____

____

____

____

____

____

____

____

Day 11 of the 21 Day Laughter Challenge

Date: ____________________

What challenged your equilibrium today? What was your attitude? How did you over come it? Was it easy it lighten up? How did your family react? What did you learn today?

Day 12 of the 21 Day Laughter Challenge

Date: ____________________

What challenged your equilibrium today? What was your attitude? How did you over come it? Was it easy it lighten up? How did your family react? What did you learn today?

Day 13 of the 21 Day Laughter Challenge

Date: ____________________

What challenged your equilibrium today? What was your attitude? How did you over come it? Was it easy it lighten up? How did your family react? What did you learn today?

____

____

____

____

____

____

____

____

____

____

____

____

____

____

Day 14 of the 21 Day Laughter Challenge

Date: ____________________

What challenged your equilibrium today? What was your attitude? How did you over come it? Was it easy it lighten up? How did your family react? What did you learn today?

Day 15 of the 21 Day Laughter Challenge

Date: ____________________

Wow, you are ¾ of the way! What dedication you are showing! Are you finding you finding your "Humor Bone"? What are you finding easy? What are you finding difficult?

What challenged your equilibrium today? What was your attitude? How did you over come it? Was it easy it lighten up? How did your family react? What did you learn today?

____

____

____

____

____

____

____

____

____

____

____

____

Day 16 of the 21 Day Laughter Challenge

Date: ____________________

What challenged your equilibrium today? What was your attitude? How did you over come it? Was it easy it lighten up? How did your family react? What did you learn today?

____

____

____

____

____

____

____

____

____

____

____

____

____

____

Day 17 of the 21 Day Laughter Challenge

Date: ____________________

What challenged your equilibrium today? What was your attitude? How did you over come it? Was it easy it lighten up? How did your family react? What did you learn today?

____

____

____

____

____

____

____

____

____

____

____

____

____

____

Day 18 of the 21 Day Laughter Challenge

Date: ____________________

What challenged your equilibrium today? What was your attitude? How did you over come it? Was it easy it lighten up? How did your family react? What did you learn today?

Day 19 of the 21 Day Laughter Challenge

Date: ____________________

What challenged your equilibrium today? What was your attitude? How did you over come it? Was it easy it lighten up? How did your family react? What did you learn today?

Day 20 of the 21 Day Laughter Challenge

Date: ___________________

What challenged your equilibrium today? What was your attitude? How did you over come it? Was it easy it lighten up? How did your family react? What did you learn today?

____

____

____

____

____

____

____

____

____

____

____

____

____

____

Day 21 of the 21 Day Laughter Challenge

Date: ____________________

Congratulations!

You have made great strides in adding humor and laughter into your daily life! Are you feeling like a humor champion? In what ways have you changed?

What challenged your equilibrium today? What was your attitude? How did you over come it? Was it easy it lighten up? How did your family react? What did you learn today?

Was today, Day 21 different than Day 1? How?

____

____

____

____

____

____

____

____

____

____

About the Author

Roberta Gold, R.T.C., CHP, created ***Laughter for the Health of it*** with a mission to empower everyone to have a more positive outlook by seeing the Humor instead of the horror in our wonderful world!

Roberta has developed simple ideas to foster an environment that promotes positive feelings, self worth and fun. She created ***Laughter Rocks!*** a program she brings into schools – to create a generation of happier, more resilient youth - empowering them so they have the tools to deal with bullies and difficult situations with less stress and more confidence instead of reacting with anger or violence. She is also working with parents and teachers so they can be positive role models.

Roberta is a Recreation Therapist and a Certified Humor Professional. She is a dynamic keynote and breakout speaker, parenting coach, and a humor and laughter consultant. Roberta is an active member as well as an advisor for the Humor Academy with the *Association for Applied and Therapeutic Humor* (www.aath.org)

Sign up for Roberta's free newsletter: Laughter Rocks! Tips and Tools to help you keep your cool no matter what. - www.laf4u.com

Contact Roberta Gold at:

www.laughterrocks.org www.laf4u.com

laf4u@sbcgloal.net

www.facebook.com/laflady

www.facebook.com/groups/LaughterRocks

www.linkedin.com/in/roberta-gold-r-t-c-62b0a89

Made in the USA
San Bernardino, CA
11 June 2018